# Communicating Clearly

# The Lessons Learned Series

Learn how the most accomplished leaders from around the globe have tackled their toughest challenges in the Harvard Business Press *Lessons Learned* series.

Concise and engaging, each volume in this series offers fourteen insightful essays by top leaders in industry, the public sector, and academia on the most pressing issues they've faced. The *Lessons Learned* series also offers all of the lessons in their original video format, free bonus videos, and other exclusive features on the 50 Lessons companion Web site **www.50lessons.com/communicate**.

Both in print and online, *Lessons Learned* contributors share surprisingly personal and insightful anecdotes and offer authoritative and practical advice drawn from their years of hard-won experience.

A crucial resource for today's busy executive, *Lessons Learned* gives you instant access to the wisdom and expertise of the world's most talented leaders.

## Other books in the series:

*Leading by Example*  
*Managing Change*  
*Managing Your Career*  
*Managing Conflict*  
*Starting a Business*  
*Hiring and Firing*  
*Making the Sale*  
*Executing for Results*  

*Sparking Innovation*  
*Making Strategy Work*  
*Doing Business Globally*  
*Going Green*  
*Crisis as Opportunity*  
*Weathering the Storm*  
*Motivating People*  
*Overcoming Obstacles*

## ⊰ LESSONS LEARNED ⊱

# Communicating Clearly

## LES*50*NS
www.50lessons.com/communicate

*Boston, Massachusetts*

Copyright 2009 Fifty Lessons Limited
All rights reserved

Printed in the United States of America
13 12 11 10 09    5 4 3 2 1

No part of this publication may be reproduced, stored in or introduced into a retrieval system, or transmitted, in any form, or by any means (electronic, mechanical, photocopying, recording, or otherwise), without the prior permission of the publisher. Requests for permission should be directed to permissions@hbsp.harvard.edu, or mailed to Permissions, Harvard Business School Publishing, 60 Harvard Way, Boston, Massachusetts 02163.

Library of Congress Cataloging-in-Publication Data

Communicating clearly.
    p. cm. — (Lessons learned)
  ISBN 978-1-4221-3983-7 (pbk.)
 1.  Communication in management.  2.  Business communication.  I.  Harvard Business School. Press.
  HD30.3.C629 2009
  658.4'5—dc22

# A NOTE FROM THE PUBLISHER

In partnership with 50 Lessons, a leading provider of digital media content, Harvard Business Press is pleased to offer *Lessons Learned,* a book series that showcases the trusted voices of the world's most experienced leaders. Through personal storytelling, each book in this series presents the accumulated wisdom of some of the world's best-known experts and offers insights into how these individuals think, approach new challenges, and use hard-won lessons from experience to shape their leadership philosophies. Organized thematically according to the topics at the top of managers' agendas—leadership, change management, entrepreneurship, innovation, and strategy, to name a few—each book draws from 50 Lessons' extensive video library of interviews with CEOs and other thought leaders. Here, the world's leading senior executives,

## A Note from the Publisher

academics, and business thinkers speak directly and candidly about their triumphs and defeats. Taken together, these powerful stories offer the advice you'll need to take on tomorrow's challenges.

As you read this book, we encourage you to visit **www.50lessons.com/communicate** to view videos of these lessons as well as additional bonus material on this topic. You'll find not only new ways of looking at the world, but also the tried-and-true advice you need to illuminate the path forward.

## CONTENTS

1. Sir David Bell
   **Clarity** — 1

2. Gill Rider
   **Listen, Question, and Engage Beyond the Superficial** — 6

3. Robin Ryde
   **Cut the Jargon** — 11

4. John Roberts
   **Avoid Uncertainty** — 16

5. William Harrison
   **Leaders Must Reach Out to Their People** — 21

6. William Pollard
   **Storytelling Brings Theory to Life** — 25

7. Sir John Banham
   **Communication Means Listening, Not Talking** — 29

# Contents

8. Paul Anderson
   **Matching Your Actions to Your Words** — 33

9. Sir Michael Rake
   **Repeat Your Message Simply and Consistently** — 39

10. John Lundgren
    **More Is Better** — 45

11. Sir Richard Evans
    **Beware of Communication Bottlenecks** — 48

12. Heather Loisel
    **Articulating the Value of Your Contribution** — 54

13. Laura Tyson
    **Find Your Personal Communication Style** — 60

14. Dame Anita Roddick
    **Openness** — 65

    About the Contributors — 71
    Acknowledgments — 85

## LESSON ONE

# Clarity

## Sir David Bell

*Director for People, Pearson*

COMMUNICATION involves finding ways to write simply and clearly so that people feel they are individuals, not units.

Language really matters in the way that you talk to people. It is quite extraordinary how some of the very worst letters are written by people in HR departments, who would freak if they received the letters they themselves had written. What we always try to do is write clearly, simply, and in the way

## Communicating Clearly

in which one would like to be spoken to. Very often we get carried away by all sorts of jargon in the belief that by using multiple syllables and words, we hide the reality. Well, we don't; we make it worse for people. We have started classes in which we take memos written around the company, and we say, "If you'd written it this way, it would have been one-third of the length and five times as clear."

So, you can help teach clarity. But it's partly a skill and partly an attitude of mind. It's a good test sometimes to take a memo and say, "Would I ever have spoken like this memo?" Nine times out of ten, the answer is, "Not on your life." If that's the case, then to write as you speak—simply and clearly—is very effective. If you're a publishing business and you don't do this properly, then you deserve to be hanged because you should be able to. But I don't think it just applies to publishing companies or to companies that deal with words. It really applies to everything. It's one of the things that has gone wrong in the way we treat each other. People use language very casually, and we

# Clarity

don't mean what we say. The people who work with us know we don't mean it; and we suffer, as businesses and organizations, as a result.

I think that the ways of communicating aren't all that different from what they've always been. E-mail is a great leveler. It enables anybody in the company, anywhere, to ask a question. And it's a great way for people to cut straight through to the top of the business; the pyramid can become much flatter. But e-mails aren't a substitute for personal communication. We find that the best way to communicate has always been person-to-person or one-to-a-group. When it comes to sending congratulations, it's much better to write a letter, and it's even better if you can do it longhand than by e-mail. E-mail is too easy. Everybody says, "They just did that because it was simple to say thank you; they didn't really mean it." It's making sure that the person who gets the communication thinks that we really did mean it. In the end a letter is the most effective way of writing. But the best way of all is person-to-person.

# Communicating Clearly

When I was running the *Financial Times,* we would send a Christmas card to all our pensioners. I hate Christmas cards that are signed by machines, so I signed all eight hundred of them myself. Somebody said to me that it was a complete waste of time, that no one would know whether I had signed it or not. All our pensioners, who were old printers and very difficult people who had retired—in fact, many of them had been forced to retire—came to their annual party. Three men came up to me and said, "We see you signed the Christmas card."

I asked, "How do you know that?"

And they replied, "We poured some water over it to see if the signature ran."

So, people do notice; they respond to being treated as individuals. They will put up with being shouted at and being told to do things if they feel that, at the end of the day, their boss values them as an individual. If they don't, it doesn't matter how honeyed all the words are—the company won't work. Language is an important part of that. We place a tremendous premium on that; and

# Clarity

we think people respond to it, although quite often, when you talk about it, people say, "It doesn't *matter* how you write." We don't believe that.

We think it is very, very important to be clear and simple, and to treat people as we would like to be treated—as individuals who matter. Language is important.

## TAKEAWAYS

- Language is an important part of conveying to people that they are valued as individuals.

- You can help teach clarity, but it's only partly a skill; it is also an attitude of mind.

- The best way to communicate has always been person-to-person or one-to-a-group.

## LESSON TWO

# Listen, Question, and Engage Beyond the Superficial

## Gill Rider

*Head, Civil Service Capability Group
Cabinet Office, UK*

LISTENING IS A vital skill in the business world because it enables you to really understand what somebody is saying, what

## Listen, Question, and Engage

they're feeling, and what they're wanting. Very often, if you listen hard, you'll find something that you didn't actually know that is very important to you.

I once went to a client with a much younger executive after we'd done some research that we really wanted to explore with the client. We went in and had a very good session; we presented our ideas, and we had a bit of a discussion. We came out afterward, and I just kicked myself, because I realized that actually what we had done was talk. We talked at the client, and every now and then he'd been polite and said something. We hadn't learned anything. So, I absolutely believe that it's very important that you listen and ask questions much more than you talk in any dialogue. I think it was Mark Twain who said something along the lines that basically you have two ears and one mouth, and you should use them proportionately.

One of the things I find really helpful that I do now whenever I'm going with a group of people to a client or into any

## Communicating Clearly

situation, is to ask them in advance, "What are you trying to achieve? What are the objectives of the meeting?" Very often people will just go into "tell" mode. They'll tell you that they're going to do this; they're going to do that. I say, "Well, stop. Think. Why don't you change all of that into the questions you want to ask the individual we are going to meet, so that you engage them in a dialogue? In doing that you'll learn a lot more than you will by just thrusting the messages at them."

It's very easy when you go into situations to have either some explicit or just unwritten assumptions in your head about what's going on in the situation. It's key that you don't let those assumptions blind you, because people will very often do the obvious. They'll say, "Oh yes, that's very interesting," and they don't mean it at all. You need to get beyond that by asking questions.

So, if somebody says to you that it's very interesting, say, "What is it exactly you find interesting in that?" so that you're always probing beyond the superficial response.

### Listen, Question, and Engage

When you're listening to somebody, if you're really engaging with them, you pick up loads of little signals from their body language about what they're really thinking. You ask questions that probe more deeply rather than just accepting the obvious. Very often people say one thing when you know that there's a different conversation going on in their head. You need to ask questions to get beneath the obvious answers.

## TAKEAWAYS

- Don't let either explicit or unwritten assumptions blind you to what's really being communicated in a given situation.

- Identify meeting objectives and intended outcomes in advance in order to frame questions that will engage the

## Communicating Clearly

people you're meeting with in a dialogue.

⚱ When you're listening to somebody, if you're really engaging with them, you'll pick up signals from their body language about what they're really thinking.

## LESSON THREE

# Cut the Jargon

## Robin Ryde

*Former Chief Executive and Principal,
National School of Government*

FROM WHERE I STAND, I find that the world—and in particular the business world—is becoming increasingly infused with complexity and uncertainty. Think about Shawn Fanning, the eighteen-year-old who set up Napster, the Web site that nearly brought the music industry to its knees. That happened largely because the music industry didn't see the potential threat.

# Communicating Clearly

In the same way now, you have electricity providers producing gas and insurance companies that can resolve all of your claims without reference to a single form; it's all done over the phone. These are things that we couldn't have imagined a few years ago and that have taken us all by surprise. In this modern world, where uncertainty and complexity are part of the furniture for us, we have to become better and better at being clear about what we're trying to say so that people can immediately grasp what we're trying to communicate.

I recently visited a school in London's East End. It was beginning to be turned around, but it was a failing school. I introduced people in the school to a bunch of senior individuals from the private and public sectors. Our role was to visit the school, to get a feel about the way that it was working, and to be part of the process of helping to turn it around. We spent some time talking to the teachers and the headmaster, as well as quite a bit of time with various pupils in the school. At one point,

## Cut the Jargon

we walked into a classroom midway through a class. They halted the class, and we introduced ourselves one by one, saying our names and what we were there to talk about, as well as what we wanted to learn about how the school was getting on and how they felt about it.

We finished our introductions, and one of the pupils asked, "But who are you?" We answered by saying that we were from the National Health Service, or HSBC, or whatever company. We then said what we were responsible for, whether it was resourcing and deployment or policy development. There was a hush after we'd done that, and the same people said, "But what do you *do*?" The same kind of iteration went on. After about five minutes, we appreciated that we hadn't conveyed at all what we were doing. They had no idea what we were about, and we'd fallen back on a jargonistic, more familiar notion of what we did in our jobs.

It struck me then as a crystal clear point: you cannot just communicate in a way that

## Communicating Clearly

has become familiar to you, or in a way that no longer has currency in the world or among the people you're talking to. We went to that school to teach the people there some lessons about how to turn it around. What we learned was that it's absolutely vital to be able to communicate clearly and in a way that your audience understands.

A leader's role is about communicating clearly to create clarity around what he's dealing with. Some people understand information very conceptually, while others understand it in very practical, down-to-earth terms. I try to anticipate the terms on which people prefer to communicate from the way in which I engage with them. There's no point in my talking about conceptual matters to people who are very practically minded; they immediately turn off—I can see it in their eyes—and I have to retreat. It's not only about speaking clearly; it's also about tailoring what you say to the way in which people take in information. We can become very quickly attuned to what others take to be interesting. We can try to touch on those things and speak in ways that can have an effect on them.

## TAKEAWAYS

- ⚐ You cannot just communicate in a way that has become familiar to you, or in a way that no longer has currency among the people you're talking to.

- ⚐ It's absolutely vital to be able to communicate clearly and in a way your audience understands.

- ⚐ Communication is not only about speaking clearly; it's also about tailoring what you say to the way in which people take in information.

## LESSON FOUR

# Avoid Uncertainty

## John Roberts

*Former CEO, United Utilities*

IN EARLY 1996 I was recruited to become the chief executive of an electricity company that had recently been taken over by another utility that happened to be its geographic neighbor. I arrived to find a senior management team that was, to say the least, demoralized because they'd been through a hostile takeover and they'd lost; there was

## Avoid Uncertainty

obviously a huge amount of concern about what would happen. I was faced with two challenges as chief executive.

On the one hand, I had to take cost out of the business because, in part, that was driving the takeover. By putting these businesses together, there were synergies that could be realized. But on the other hand, I had to take this group of demoralized people, turn it around, and start to get the business to perform. That was a significant challenge.

I met the people on day one, all eighty of them, and could very rapidly sense their worries, their concerns. They didn't know what was going to happen to them. I decided that the best way forward was to be absolutely upfront and honest with them. So, I gave everybody a promise that within four weeks, they would know exactly what was going to happen to them. And I saw each individual, worked through what parts of the organization we would keep, what parts we would not need because of the integration; and then I kept my word and told everybody what was

# Communicating Clearly

going to happen. Some people would have to go; some people were going to stay.

Interestingly, for the people who were going to leave, once I said to them, "I'm sorry, but there is no room for you in this organization going forward. However, we will do all we can to help you find another job: we will give you time to go and look for a job, anything we can do in terms of references and other assistance, a good financial package—but the key thing is, on this date, you will leave," almost without exception people said yes, there was regret that they were going to go and leave colleagues they'd been with for some time and an organization that they'd very much enjoyed working for. But once I told them exactly what was going to happen to them, the overwhelming emotion that came back was a sense of relief. At least I know what's going to happen to me now. I can plan for the future; I'm going to move on, and I can work around that.

When you say to people, "Well, I'm not really certain. We'll give it six months, and then we'll have another look," you really put into their minds a huge amount of

# Avoid Uncertainty

uncertainty. Should I go? Should I stay? And that is a hugely negative emotion. It really, really damages them, and I've seen this borne out many times subsequently. This is the first time I'd experienced it with such a large group of people, and once we'd made those decisions and it was very clear who was going, who was staying, what was going on, and that we also dealt with the consequences of our decisions in a very humane kind of way, morale picked up. Amazingly, morale really started to rise and, going forward, we built on that basis, and business performance improved quite significantly over the next several months.

The key lesson is that if you are absolutely honest with people, if you make your decisions effectively and quickly, and make them for all the right business reasons, but then implement them and communicate them quickly, clearly, and humanely and deal with the consequences humanely, then people will go with what you're doing, understand what you're doing, and you get the best result. If you have a confused message—if you're indecisive, uncertain—that just sows

## Communicating Clearly

the seeds of uncertainty, doubt, and anxiety, and then you have a very demoralized workforce. And that feeds through into performance.

## TAKEAWAYS

- Uncertainty about the future is a negative emotion that can be very damaging to people.

- People can feel regret about moving on from a company while also feeling relief that their course of action is clear.

- People will understand and cooperate with business decisions more effectively if you are honest, humane, and swift in communicating those decisions and acting on them.

## LESSON FIVE

# Leaders Must Reach Out to Their People

## William Harrison

*Former Chairman of the Board,
JPMorgan Chase &. Co.*

THIS IS A LESSON learned about communication for me as a leader—as CEO of JP Morgan at that time—and it was around the 9/11 tragedy. We had a lot of people downtown who saw everything, who

## Communicating Clearly

experienced a lot of what happened in a very real way; we lost a person; and then we had another hundred thousand people around the world and in other places in New York who, like the rest of the world, were shocked by this and were going through a very emotional challenge.

Some of my staff came in and told me, "Bill, you should go out with a very personal voice mail tomorrow morning, trying to reach out to people because people need an emotional connection here. They are looking for leaders to speak out and embrace what's happened and why." So, I said that I'd be very happy to do that—wasn't sure it was a great idea—but I thought it was certainly okay. And they said, "The second thing we want you to do—we recommend you do—is go down to the Chase Building where we have two or three thousand people who come to work every day and stand there and greet people one by one as they come in."

So, the next morning I went on voice mail, out to a hundred thousand people, and I tried to reach out to them as best I

## Leaders Must Reach Out

could and share my feelings in a very personal way. And then the next morning I went down and greeted over two or three thousand people personally, as they came in the office building one at a time, and I thanked them for going to work that day because everybody wasn't going to work that day; they were in such shock.

Now the result of all of that was surprising to me. I tend to be a pretty pragmatic guy, so I didn't anticipate the impact of this, but I got an enormous number of e-mails and feedback from everyone about the value of my doing that. And the result was that it sensitized me a lot more than I had been to the value of communication from leaders. And while we all do a fair amount of communicating, after that experience, I really ramped up our whole communication strategy in terms of trying to constantly go out and reach all of our people in a lot of different ways.

Again, there's a very simple lesson but a very powerful lesson about communicating: if there's ever any

### Communicating Clearly

doubt about communicating, err on the side of overcommunicating because people want to be communicated to.

## TAKEAWAYS

- ⚑ Visible leadership can have a tremendous impact on an organization, its people, and the leader himself.

- ⚑ From their lone position, it is easy for leaders to underestimate the impact and value of personal communications.

- ⚑ When in doubt, leaders should err on the side of overcommunicating because people want to be communicated to.

## LESSON SIX

# Storytelling Brings Theory to Life

## William Pollard

*Chairman Emeritus, ServiceMaster*

I THINK THERE IS A continuing problem for all of us in replicating lessons throughout our organization, especially one that is growing larger and more diverse. In our situation, we grew to serving not only customers here in the United States but also

## Communicating Clearly

in forty-five foreign countries. One of the ways I think we can do it is for the senior officers to continue to spend most of their time out of the office, touching the business at what I call strategic intercept points. And when you do something—when you physically do something that's significant within an organization—the organization talks about it. You have all kinds of channels in the organization repeating it.

I can remember once when I was taking my We Serve day at the call center, listening to customers complain about our pest-control service. This one call came in, and it was a customer complaining because we were sending him a bill. He was saying that we hadn't done the job. So, I linked our local branch manager in to that call, and our branch manager was responding to the customer in a very tough way—"We're going to sue you if you don't pay this bill; it's five months old . . ." He didn't know who I was at this point. But on our screens it also showed that this customer was a termite customer, and frankly we earn a lot more profit

## Storytelling Brings Theory to Life

from termite work than we do from pest-control work.

I was sitting there thinking, this branch manager is destroying our relationship with this customer. And I couldn't help myself; I said over the phone, "Look at all we're doing for this customer," and then the branch manager changed his tone a little bit. Finally, when it was all finished, the branch manager called the head of the call center and said, "Who was that person you have answering the telephone? Why was he telling me to look at the whole customer?" And then, when the head of the call center said, "Well, it was Bill Pollard, the CEO of the company," that story rippled throughout Terminix.

But it focused us again on who the customer was.

So, in my experience, storytelling makes the intangible tangible. Often when you're talking about management concepts or theories, you're talking about something that's intangible. But when you can relate the intangible to a factual situation, when people

### Communicating Clearly

can see it in the way you conduct yourself, it has reality, it has application, and learning comes from application in reality.

## TAKEAWAYS

- Replicating lessons learned throughout an organization becomes more challenging the larger and more diverse that organization becomes.

- When you physically do something that's significant within an organization, the organization talks about it and amplifies it.

- Storytelling makes the intangible tangible.

## LESSON SEVEN

# Communication Means Listening, Not Talking

## Sir John Banham

*Chairman, Johnson Matthey*

COMMUNICATION IS about listening, not talking.

Years ago I found myself sitting next to Nelson Mandela on his first visit to London after he had been let out of Robben Island prison. He'd been in jail for twenty-five

## Communicating Clearly

years. Then, as now, he was probably one of the three most instantly recognizable people on Earth, behind the Pope and the president of the United States. If he walked down the street, everyone would know exactly who he was. I sat next to him for an hour, and this great man did not use the word "I" once. He was the most aggressive listener I have ever sat next to, and it was an astonishing experience.

He spent all his time asking me about what was going on in East Germany because I'd just come back from Dresden. I was explaining how things had changed after the fall of the Berlin Wall. I wondered why he was asking me all these questions. It turned out that all the economic advice the African National Congress was receiving came from former East German economics professors. He wanted to know whether he should listen to what they were saying. It had come as a huge shock to absolutely everybody that what had been a very successful economy on paper was, in fact, a basket case—economically, environmentally, socially, morally, and politically.

## Communication Means Listening

What this great man was doing was listening. I doubt very much whether you can remember a single sound bite that Mandela has produced in the millions and millions of words written about him. But I would be very surprised if anyone couldn't conjure up in their mind's eye Nelson Mandela in a Springbok rugby shirt. He was handing the rugby World Cup to the captain of the South African team, the Springboks, which represented all that he had fought against for twenty-seven years.

The moral of the story is that communication is not about talking. Too many people believe that communication is about talking, but it's about listening. In business it's about listening to your customers and your staff. When businesses have gone horribly off the track, it's because their chief executives have been talking, giving interviews, and believing their own publicity; they've forgotten that their job is to listen, not to talk. Communication—at minimum—is a two-way street, and for me it's more about listening than talking. Nelson Mandela taught me that lesson twenty years ago,

### Communicating Clearly

and I can't think of a better person from whom to learn a lesson.

## TAKEAWAYS

- Communication is about listening, not talking.

- A leader's actions are far more memorable than his words.

- In business, communication is about listening to your customers and your employees.

## LESSON EIGHT

# Matching Your Actions to Your Words

## Paul Anderson

*Chairman, Spectra Energy*

AFTER I SPENT about a year at BHP Billiton, the company was really getting back on track, and all the measures of success were pretty positive. Certainly, profitability was up, and our efficiency was up; we were getting great productivity. You could look at

## Communicating Clearly

almost any measure, and it was positive. Except safety. Safety had actually gone down a little bit.

I was very vexed by this, and I kept asking the head of the safety group, "What is it? Why isn't the organization embracing a safety culture, and why can't we seem to improve our safety performance?"

After beating round the bush for a while, he finally blurted it out. He said, "Well, you're the problem."

I said, "I'm the problem? I'm a real proponent of safety; we've got it right in our charter; I can't imagine a higher objective for the company; I can't imagine anything going before it."

He said, "Well, you're a lousy role model—just look at what you're doing."

I replied, "Lousy role model—what do you mean?"

He said, "You know, people notice that when you come to work you jaywalk across the street; you don't go to the corner. People notice that when you're out visiting a plant, if you're wearing dark safety glasses

## Matching Your Actions to Your Words

and you come inside, you take off the dark glasses even if you don't have a pair of clear safety glasses to replace them with and you're still in an area where you need them. They notice that when you go up and down steps you don't hold onto the handrail, which is the standard practice we have here. They notice that you don't park your car backward in a parking space, which, again, is the safety standard that we have. You're just basically a lousy role model."

Of course, that took me a little aback. But he went on and said, "When you go to visit a manager, the first thing you ask is, 'How are you doing against budget?' You start asking financial questions; you don't start with, 'How is your safety program? What results have you had over the last year? What are your two or three safety issues that you have here?' So, people assume you're not particularly interested in safety. And in fact, they're focusing on everything but safety because you really haven't highlighted it."

That really struck me. I had never been in a situation where I was so clearly scrutinized

## Communicating Clearly

as a role model and where safety was so important, because this was primarily a mining operation and steel mills, and very much an industrial setting. I realized that not only was I being scrutinized on the job, but also I was being scrutinized off it, too. One of the things that the head of the safety group said was, "People know you don't like to wear a helmet when you ride a motorcycle." And I thought, "Well, what's that got to do with anything?" But if you don't display these values in your personal life, then you obviously don't really embrace the values. It really drove home the point. Somebody once said, "Good leadership is doing the right thing, even when no one's looking." I realized that, actually, somebody *is* looking. It wasn't the case that no one was looking.

So, I really took that to heart, and there's a good ending to this story because once I realized how important it was to establish myself as a good role model, I took it on as a personal passion to improve the safety program there—to get personally involved, to set myself up as role model—and it really

## Matching Your Actions to Your Words

had an impact on the organization. The stats got bigger, and it was very gratifying to me because when you have fifty thousand people, a slight improvement in the stats is actually a huge reduction in human suffering in terms of what actually happens out there in the field. In fact, when I came to Duke Energy, the first thing I did was look at the safety program and start talking safety because I realized the impact that you have at the top, and the fact that you are the role model, has a huge impact on what the organization is going to do.

The key point that I really got out of that experience was that you are a role model 100 percent of the time. When you're the CEO of a company, you can't separate your personal life from your professional life. People learn what you do in your personal life; they follow what's going on; they watch you in situations where you might even think you're not being watched. And if you don't walk the talk, they pick that up in a heartbeat. They sense very quickly whether your words and your actions are

### Communicating Clearly

tied together, and if you don't match your words with your actions, the organization basically discards your words.

## TAKEAWAYS

- Leaders are role models whose behavior has a huge impact on organizational behavior.

- When you're the leader of a company, you can't separate your personal life from your professional life; you are a role model 100 percent of the time.

- People in an organization sense very quickly whether a leader's words and actions are tied together; and if they don't match, the organization will discard the words.

## LESSON NINE

# Repeat Your Message Simply and Consistently

## Sir Michael Rake

*Chairman, BT Group*

ONE OF THE THINGS a leader has to do in today's world is be a very strong communicator. He has to be very, very effective at communicating internally and, in many cases, communicating externally. That's a major part of his role, and to do it he has to

## Communicating Clearly

do a number of things: simplify the message, make it clear, and make it consistent. And one thing that is really difficult to do is to recognize you have to endlessly repeat it.

You can't assume because you've said it once or twice, or because you wrote it in a brochure, you sent an e-mail, or it's in the strategy document, that people—even if they have read or heard it—have understood it or that it's deeply ingrained within them. You have to continuously repeat what your strategy is, what the issues are in simple terms, and never believe that people will say, "My goodness, I've heard this too many times."

People find it difficult to understand continuous changes in strategy and direction, unless they're necessary. Yes, they can understand the need to know, in a very simple way, the general direction they're going in so they can get behind it. And they can understand that things might change—the wind may blow and you may have to change course slightly—but you still have an objective; you have a clear objective of where

## Repeat Your Message Simply

you're going and you continuously say what that objective is.

One of the things that made me understand this is that I started to get involved with our firms when we were moving from fairly complex partnership structures to try and bring our firm much more closely together and get a much more aligned strategy on a pan-European as well as a pan-U.K. level. You realize that having once made a presentation on the issues, which were clear and concise and seemed to be understood, you'd go and visit an office or a country three weeks or a month later, and everyone was asking the same questions you'd already answered, because what you were saying hadn't really registered. And you had to say it again and again and again.

I think you also have to know that as a leader of an organization, particularly a large one, people . . . will take the sayings of a leader in vain. In other words, people will attribute comments or strategies to a leader more broadly than he intended them. Therefore it is very important that

## Communicating Clearly

the leader is heard to say what he actually says, in a very simple way, so that he can't be misreported or misinterpreted second- or thirdhand. It really struck me that even if you say it seven, eight, ten, a hundred times, eventually you stop and they get it—but it takes a lot of repetition. If you remember to keep it simple, keep it consistent, get your message clear, simplify things, and repeat them endlessly, what you see is that it works.

I remember, when our firm started—I guess in 1997 or 1998—to really come together and integrate into one partnership, many people would say at the beginning, "You're crazy; you can't do this! Culturally this is too difficult." Four years later, it's not an issue for anyone, and they ask, "Why did we do anything differently?" It wasn't anything very clever or sophisticated. It was endlessly repeating and reminding people why we were doing it—because people got that, people saw the benefits that they could obtain, they saw it coming through, and suddenly it's happened.

## Repeat Your Message Simply

Making things simple, in whatever line of business you're in, is one of the biggest challenges. You know when you watch somebody who's a fantastic athlete or a high wire artist that it looks amazingly simple—but it's not. I think the same thing applies.

One of the things that we look for in our firm in terms of the best professionals are the people who can take really, really complex situations, simplify them, and explain them simply to a sophisticated audience. That's really important, and it's part of what makes somebody able to communicate effectively. It's the same whether you're an adviser dealing with a board, whether you're a politician dealing with your audience, or whether you're a chief executive dealing with the strategy of an organization to your board or to your employees. That ability to bring complex things, simplify them, and present them so people can understand you is a very important part of your armory.

**Communicating Clearly**

## TAKEAWAYS

- In today's world, a leader must be a strong, effective communicator, both internally and externally.

- To be an effective communicator, leaders must simplify their message, make it clear and consistent, and counterintuitively recognize that they must endlessly repeat it.

- An effective communicator can take complex situations, simplify them, and explain them simply to a sophisticated audience.

## LESSON TEN

# More Is Better

## John Lundgren

*Chairman and CEO, The Stanley Works*

COMMUNICATION IS GOOD, and you can't do too much of it. Specifically, in good times it is important, regardless of the size of the organization or the group, to share the successes and to smell the roses. And it is not that important how it is done. Organizations of different cultures and different sizes may do it differently: with a simple verbal comment, a handwritten

## Communicating Clearly

note, a small trophy, or a dinner. But that is the easy part—sharing the success.

I think what's more important is in bad times, or in times of crisis, to step communications up to a level two, three, or four times what might normally be ongoing. Because, while it may sound pessimistic, in my experience—having worked many years in the United States and then thirteen years abroad both in continental Europe and in the United Kingdom—with a lack of specific information during bad times, people assume the worst. So, by stepping up the communications, explaining, answering questions—in a written form or electronically, and, most importantly, face-to-face, if it can be done—the ultimate impact is that communication increases trust.

At Georgia-Pacific we did an employee survey every year, and we found a direct correlation between the frequency of communication and how people felt about what they were doing. Eighty to 95 percent of the people actually felt good about what they were doing, and what they were doing in

## More Is Better

particular had an impact on a customer. Those are really high numbers. In addition to trust, morale, and things of that nature, you'd include the productivity as well.

So, communicating is just a simple, sound, intelligent thing to do, which has positive results on morale and positive results on your bottom line.

## TAKEAWAYS

- Stepping up communications, particularly in bad times or times of crisis, increases trust within an organization.

- A direct correlation exists between the frequency of communication and how people feel about what they're doing.

- Frequent communication has a positive effect on productivity as well as morale.

## ⊰ LESSON ELEVEN ⊱

# Beware of Communication Bottlenecks

## Sir Richard Evans

*Chairman, United Utilities*

IN MANY WAYS you can't deliver good leadership without having good communication, and communication is a part of leadership. Although you clearly need to have processes by which you are able to force communication through an

## Beware of Communication Bottlenecks

organization, you will never get high-quality leadership unless you have good-quality communication.

The problem in most organizations is that it's very difficult for the guys at the top to communicate throughout the organization and get to the guys at the bottom. Somebody once described the problems in communication to me in the most wonderful way. That person said, "Making changes work in an organization, and therefore making communication work in an organization, is a bit like passing liquid through a very fine claret bottle. You have a very narrow neck on the bottle, and then the shoulders of the bottle come out, and you have a large volume under the neck at the bottom."

His analogy was that the management sat in the neck of the bottle. The rest of the people who worked in the organization were sitting under the shoulders of the bottle, down in the area of the bottle where the biggest volume was contained. The biggest challenge for the guy at the top to overcome in order to communicate with the guys at

## Communicating Clearly

the bottom all resided in the neck of the bottle, and—lo and behold!—who occupies this space but the management? So, the biggest obstacle to communicating inside an organization is the management itself. Until you can find a way of getting all those guys to share your view in terms of communication, these people will always be an obstacle. That's why it's so important to get the right guys into the neck of the bottle: people who actually want to share your views on how to get down and do that sort of communicating.

If you look at the companies that do this successfully, they have cracked that problem. It's a human reaction: "Knowledge actually is power. If I keep the knowledge to myself, in some way, a degree of power resides in me that somebody else inside the organization doesn't have." Now if all that knowledge is sitting in the neck of the bottle, and it isn't being shared, even with the other guys in the neck of the bottle, how the hell can it ever be shared across the whole of the organization?

## Beware of Communication Bottlenecks

The answer is that it never can, so you somehow have to find a way—and it's sometimes quite a brutal process—of ensuring that the right guys occupy the neck of the bottle. Anybody who is not capable of sharing information, can't work in a team, or is unable to make sure that there's a very short communication process between the top and the bottom of the organization, needs to get onto *The Times*' classified pages ASAP because they are never going to add value to the business.

The best way is to have a very short communication chain, whereby you can get information from the top to the bottom in the shortest time possible. That is always best achieved by using the organization that you have. It's a lot better for a guy at a particular level of the organization to be able to get the communication from the guy he works for. So, the job of the people at the top has to be to make sure that chain will work. If you do it really successfully, even in a very big organization—providing you have a decent management structure

### Communicating Clearly

without too many layers in it—there's absolutely no reason why it shouldn't. If I was chief executive of a company and I wanted to get a message out at nine o'clock, there's absolutely no reason at all why that message should not have gotten around to even a hundred thousand people by lunchtime.

## TAKEAWAYS

- You can't deliver good leadership without having good communication, and communication is a part of leadership.

- In order to facilitate communication throughout an entire organization, it is essential to have people who share your views of communication.

## Beware of Communication Bottlenecks

⚑ Anyone who is not capable of sharing information, cannot work in a team, or is not able to support a very short communication process between the top and the bottom of the organization will always be an obstacle to communication and therefore leadership.

## LESSON TWELVE

# Articulating the Value of Your Contribution

## Heather Loisel

*VP, Global Marketing Operations, SAP AG*

THERE HAS TO BE a constant drive to figure out what you're doing in delivering value to an organization. You have to be able to answer that question. If you can't answer that question, then you don't know. If you don't know, then you're incapable of

## Articulating the Value

building a case for why you should stick around.

When you move from a line position to a staff position, you want to make sure that you are quantifying what you're doing. You will, in fact, differentiate yourself from your peers. There are a lot of people who work hard, care a lot, and do the right thing, but when you ask them at the end of the day, "What have you done to help drive the value of the company or to achieve the objectives of the company?" their ability to articulate it or not makes them different. Let's look at some of the hard decisions that people have to make.

One of the hard decisions that people have to make is, "Do you get money, or do I? Do you stay on when a company's going through reduction in force, or do I?" Your ability to articulate what you've done for the company and what the value of that is to the company, based on the company's objectives and strategies, differentiates you from the people who can't. When you wake up in the morning, regardless of what role you're in,

## Communicating Clearly

if you don't know what you're doing to contribute to the end game in a positive way, what you're doing to help the objectives, and you can't articulate it, you're at risk.

There's a core principle that people always need to understand how what they're doing affects the outcome. That's not in a bad way. It's not just risk mitigation against, "I don't want to be the one laid off." It's also an exciting way to look at what you're doing. But how do you do it in a way that you're not the kid in the classroom saying, "Look at me! Look what I did!"? That's not really what you want to do here. There are a couple ways to articulate what value you're contributing to the organization in a positive way versus a negative way.

One positive way to share is, "I'm just excited about it." If somebody comes up to me and says, "Heather, how was your day?" I say, "Today was awesome, because from a marketing operations standpoint, we found a way to take the marketing funnel conversion rates and apply them to the business so that a marketer can tell how effective his or

## Articulating the Value

her campaigns are. I'm excited about that because that's a cool thing to be able to do. It means when we spend a dollar on marketing, we're going to know what happened to it. And if we know what happened to it, then we can figure out how to optimize it." It's a lot like when you're listening to a radio and you don't like the station or the volume; you turn the knobs and something happens. By being able to articulate the value of what you're doing, you're saying, "I'm going to turn the knob. I turned the knob, and this happened." That's an exciting thing when you're talking about why you are spending money in resources.

Another way to articulate your value to the organization is to communicate what you're doing, why you're doing it, and then just follow up. *Follow up.* I know a lot of people who spend an extraordinary amount of time working hard all day long, and they never take a moment and say, "What did I do?" It's okay on a quarterly basis to go to your boss and say, "Here's what I did, and here's what I'm going to do." He'll

## Communicating Clearly

appreciate that. That's not tooting your own horn; that's simply saying, "This is what I got accomplished, and this is what I'm going to do next quarter. What do you think? Is it good or is it bad? Am I doing the right things? Could I be doing something better?" It delivers value to that manager, to whomever you're working for. I don't care if it's a CEO: "Here's what we're going to do; here's what we did. Are we on the right track?"

## TAKEAWAYS

- If you can't articulate what you're doing to deliver value to an organization, then you can't build a case for why you should stick around.

- Your ability to articulate what you've done for the company and what the

## Articulating the Value

value of that is to the company, based on the company's objectives and strategies, differentiates you from the people who can't.

⚜ Articulate your value by sharing your excitement about what you're doing, communicating what you're doing to your manager, and asking whether you're doing the right things.

## LESSON THIRTEEN

# Find Your Personal Communication Style

## Laura Tyson

*National Economic Adviser to President Clinton*

REGARDING THE CONCEPT of "chief executive officer," when you say C-E-O, the "E," I often think, should stand for *explaining* rather than *executing*, because

## Find Your Personal Style

so much of leadership at a business level is about communication and explaining, and engaging in motivating through explanation.

Communication has always been a part of my life. I've come out of an academic tradition; I was a professor. I understood the importance of communication, but I think it was most clarified for me as a leader when I first arrived in Washington. I was appointed as President Clinton's chief economic adviser. One of the responsibilities of that post is to essentially be a voice for the economic policy of the administration. And that voice has to go through many different audiences—through congressional testimony; dealing with the media, both television and print; and many private sector groups, whether it's the National Chamber of Commerce or a local community group that deals with, say, poverty in New Orleans. You are constantly put on stage to communicate, explain, and motivate support for the president's economic policy.

## Communicating Clearly

I realized this was a key part of the job, and I also found that my ability to do it rested really on three things—first of all, understanding the content, knowing exactly what I should be saying in a situation. I really believe that in order to communicate, engage, or explain, you need to know the content. You also need to know yourself.

When I went before Congress the first time, it was a very unnerving experience, because it was highly political, and I was going to be attacked by those who didn't believe in President Clinton's economic policy and excoriated for being a big-spending democrat, etc. I certainly had content, because I was a professional economist and my questioners were not, but I also understood the audience. I think that was a very important part. I knew that my role would be to, on the one hand, mobilize those who could work with us, and on the other hand, at least give those who were against us some sense that the issue had been seriously thought through.

The last thing is just style of presentation. It's very important for people to realize what

### Find Your Personal Style

their natural style is. For example, I'm not a comedian. I don't tell jokes. I don't consider myself a guru. I'm not there to entertain in a kind of very energizing way. I'm there to explain; I'm there to take economic concepts and make them simple and compelling.

I believe strongly in the value of communication as an important leadership skill. The three things that came out of my congressional experience, my briefing the president experience, and my briefing community groups experience, are to have the content easily at your disposal, know the audience—because there are different audiences with different needs—and know your own style.

## TAKEAWAYS

- In order to communicate, engage, or explain anything, you need to understand the content.

## Communicating Clearly

- ⊱ You need to understand your audience, how they will receive your content, and your role in relation to them.

- ⊱ In addition you need to know yourself and understand your own personal style.

## ⊰ LESSON FOURTEEN ⊱

# Openness

## Dame Anita Roddick

*Founder, The Body Shop International*

IN BUSINESS I LEARNED that there's a language of secrecy; there's a language of noncommunication. Whether it's the board or the executive committee, there isn't the communication right down to the troops.

When I set up The Body Shop and it started to become less of a livelihood and more of a business, one of the things that I wanted was openness and transparency everywhere, and I didn't want anybody—any

## Communicating Clearly

group, any management—to be a hindrance. One of the best things we did was to hand out a booklet when you joined The Body Shop, which said, "This is what this company is about; this is what its mission is; this is its beliefs." Within this book were six or seven red envelopes. Any time you were really upset about anything the organization had done, or the people or the founders had done, you wrote a note and put it into the red envelope, and it was sent to me; and I had to respond belly-to-belly with you within twenty-four hours. Brilliant. Use lavatory walls. We used to write messages on the lavatory walls to say, for example: "Is this a family-friendly company?" Good questions appeared.

People were always allowed to write anonymously, and the board had to respond at the same time. The board hated doing that, but I learned various techniques for getting openness in the company. I had a little newspaper called *Gobsmacked*. All the mistakes, all the screw-ups, all the great ideas would always be in this little journal

## Openness

that we would always send straight down to the shops; because it was they who met the customers, not the people who were in management. So, the communication line to the shops was there.

I think it's really important to be open because there's a terrorism of perfection that you're doing this type of stuff, and it has to be perfect. But it's a journey about which no books have been written. There's not a book on how to deal with the Kayapo Indians in the middle of the Amazon, or in Ghana, in Kumasi; there's no book that deals with that. It really, really taught me that, for anything you do, if you tell your customers that "This is a journey," "We're two steps forward, and we'll be one step back," or "We screwed up here," and if you can use that language in a continuous story, there's something so open and so honest that there's a sort of a grace to it.

We think that everything has to be perfect when we talk about a company. But companies are not made by Nature, they're not

### Communicating Clearly

ordained by God or the gods, or both. They are about human beings who are fragile and flawed. But if you have within yourself a sense of purpose and an empathy with the human condition, and if you can communicate that, then I think people are incredibly forgiving.

## TAKEAWAYS

- ⚜ Commitment from senior management to open, personal, and prompt responses to employee concerns and feedback is a powerful way to bring openness to a company.

- ⚜ Openness and transparency in communication mitigate the terrorism of perfection many people labor under when conducting business.

## Openness

⚏ If you have within yourself a sense of purpose and an empathy with the human condition, and if you can communicate that, then people will be incredibly forgiving of your mistakes.

# ABOUT THE CONTRIBUTORS

**Paul Anderson** is the Chairman of Spectra Energy. He is also a Director of Qantas Airways and BHP Billiton, a global resources company.

Mr. Anderson started his career at Ford Motor Company, holding various positions from 1969 to 1972. He was Planning Manager from 1972 until 1977, and then joined PanEnergy. Over the ensuing years, he served in various leadership roles within PanEnergy, culminating in becoming its Chairman, President, and CEO.

In 1998 Mr. Anderson moved to BHP, where he was Managing Director and CEO until its merger with Billiton in 2001. He then became Managing Director and CEO of BHP Billiton until his retirement from the company in 2002.

Mr. Anderson returned to Duke Energy as Chairman and CEO in November 2003. He became Chairman of Spectra Energy in 2007 when Duke Energy's natural gas business was spun off into a new company called Spectra Energy.

**Sir John Banham** has been Chairman of Johnson Matthey, leader in advanced materials technology, since April 2006. He is also Chairman of Spacelabs

# About the Contributors

Medical, Inc., a medical device and services company.

He started his career in the Foreign Office in 1962 before moving to Reed International, where he became Director of Marketing. In 1969, he joined the management consulting firm McKinsey & Company, becoming a Principal in 1975 and the youngest British Director of the firm in 1980. Sir John set up the Audit Commission in 1983 and became Director General of the Confederation of British Industry from 1987 to 1992.

He was the Chairman of Westcountry Television from the company's founding in June 1992 until it was sold to Carlton Communications in December 1996. He then became Chairman of Kingfisher Plc. from 1996 to December 2001. Additionally, he was at the helm of Tarmac from February 1994 until March 2000.

Sir John was Chairman of Whitbread from 2000 to 2005 and also Chairman of Geest from 2002 to 2005. He is currently a Senior Independent Director of AMVESCAP and Cyclacel Pharmaceuticals, and a Director of Merchants Trust plc and Invesco.

**Sir David Bell** is a Director of Pearson, an international media company. He is also Chairman of the Financial Times Group, having been Chief Executive of the *Financial Times* since 1993.

In July 1998 Sir David was appointed Pearson's Director for People with responsibility for the

## About the Contributors

recruitment, motivation, development, and reward of employees across the Pearson Group. In addition, he is a Director of *The Economist,* the Vitec Group Plc, and The Windmill Partnership. Sir David is Chairman of Common Purpose International, Chairman of Crisis, Chairman of Sadler's Wells Foundation, and Chairman of the International Youth Foundation.

He was also Chairman of the Millennium Bridge Trust (1995–2000), which was responsible for conceiving the first new bridge across the Thames in one hundred years.

Sir David was educated at Cambridge University and the University of Pennsylvania.

**Sir Richard Evans** is the Chairman of United Utilities, a position he has held since 2001. He stepped down from the board in July 2008.

Sir Richard started his career at the Ministry of Transport and Civil Aviation. He joined the British Aircraft Corporation (BAC) and was promoted to Commercial Director of the Warton Division of British Aerospace (BAe) in 1978. In 1981 he became Deputy Managing Director for BAe Warton. Three years later he was made Deputy Managing Director of the British Aerospace Military Aircraft Division. In the following year, Sir Richard was appointed to the Board of British Aerospace as Marketing Director, and in the year after that became Chairman of the British Aerospace Defense companies.

# About the Contributors

Sir Richard was appointed CEO of British Aerospace in 1990. In 1998 he joined British Aerospace as Chairman, and continued to Chair the company when it became BAE Systems following the merger with Marconi Electronic Systems. In July 2004 he retired from the board but continues to advise the company.

In 1997 Sir Richard joined the Board of United Utilities as a Director and was appointed Chairman four years later.

**William Harrison** retired as Chairman, Director, and CEO of JPMorgan Chase & Co. in December 2006. Mr. Harrison held this title since November 2001. From January 2001 until that time, he held the position of President and CEO.

Prior to the merger with J.P. Morgan & Co., Inc., Mr. Harrison had been Chairman and CEO of the Chase Manhattan Corporation, a position he assumed in January 2000. He had held the same responsibilities at the Chemical Bank prior to its merger with Chase in 1996. In 1978 he moved to London to take responsibility for the bank's U.K. business, and in 1982 was promoted to Division Head of Europe. Mr. Harrison returned to the United States in 1983 to run the U.S. corporate division, and was put in charge of the bank's global Banking and Corporate Finance group three years later.

Mr. Harrison is a Director for Cousins Properties, Inc., and has been a Director for Merck & Co. since 1999.

# About the Contributors

**Heather Loisel** is Vice President of Global Marketing Operations, SAP AG, a leading provider of business software.

Before assuming this role, Ms. Loisel was the Vice President of Field Marketing for SAP Americas, leading the delivery of marketing content and demand generation to customers and prospects in North and Latin America. Before that she served as the Vice President of Proposal & Knowledge Management of SAP America, Inc.

Prior to joining SAP in 2003, Ms. Loisel held global leadership positions with PeopleSoft, a human resource management services provider. She also held sales, marketing, and alliances roles with CODA, Ltd. of the United Kingdom, Sterling Commerce, and CompuServe.

**John Lundgren** is the Chairman and CEO of The Stanley Works, a worldwide manufacturer and marketer of tools and hardware products. He has held the position since 2004.

Mr. Lundgren began his business career in brand management at the Gillette Company in Boston, then moved to the American Can Company's Consumer Products Division, where he was Director of Marketing when it was acquired by James River in 1982. He has held positions in finance, manufacturing, corporate development, strategic planning, and marketing in both the United States and Europe with Fort James Corporation, a leading international consumer products

## About the Contributors

company. Fort James was acquired by Georgia-Pacific Corporation in November 2000.

Mr. Lundgren also served as President of Georgia-Pacific's European Consumer Products business, where he led its strategic development and all its business operating activities.

He is on the board of the National Association of Manufacturers.

**William Pollard** is the Chairman Emeritus of the ServiceMaster Company, a company that provides service to residential and commercial customers in the United States. Mr. Pollard has been with the organization for more than thirty years, and during that time has held the role of CEO twice.

He joined ServiceMaster in 1977 and served his first term as CEO over the decade spanning from 1983 to 1993. During that period the organization experienced a major change in its structure and direction, including the rapid growth of its Consumer Group. In 1999 Mr. Pollard returned as CEO, and remained in the role for sixteen months until his successor was identified and elected. Mr Pollard was also Chairman of ServiceMaster from 1990 until April 2002, and he remains an adviser to the company.

Prior to joining ServiceMaster, Mr. Pollard was engaged in the practice of law, spending 1963 until 1972 specializing in corporate finance and tax matters. From 1972 to 1977, he served on the faculty of Wheaton College and also as its Vice President.

## About the Contributors

Mr. Pollard is a former Chairman and Director of UnumProvident Corporation. He is Chair of Central DuPage Hospital. He is Chairman of Wheaton College and the Avodah Institute, and he is a Director of the Illinois Children's Healthcare Foundation.

Mr. Pollard is also the author of *The Soul of the Firm*, and has recently released another book entitled *Serving Two Masters? Reflections on God and Profit*.

**Sir Michael Rake** is Chairman of BT Group. He is Chairman of the UK Commission for Employment and Skills, as well as a Director of Barclays Plc., the McGraw-Hill Companies, and the Financial Reporting Council. He is also Chairman of the Guidelines Monitoring Committee, a private equity oversight group. From May 2002 to September 2007, Sir Michael was Chairman of KPMG International. Prior to his appointment as Chairman of KPMG International, he was Chairman of KPMG in Europe and Senior Partner of KPMG in the United Kingdom.

He joined KPMG in 1974 and worked in Continental Europe before transferring to the Middle East to run the practice for three years in 1986. He transferred to London in 1989, became a member of the U.K. Board in 1991, and had a number of leadership roles in the United Kingdom before being elected U.K. Senior Partner in 1998.

Sir Michael is also a Vice President of the RNIB (Royal National Institute of Blind People), a

## About the Contributors

member of the Board of the TransAtlantic Business Dialogue, a member of the CBI International Advisory Board, the Chartered Management Institute, the Department of Trade and Industry's U.S./U.K. Regulatory Taskforce, the Advisory Council for Business for New Europe, the Ethnic Minority Employment Taskforce, the School of Oriental and African Studies Advisory Board, the Advisory Board of the Judge Institute at the University of Cambridge, and the Global Advisory Board of the Oxford University Centre for Corporate Reputation. He is Senior Adviser for Chatham House and an Association Member of BUPA.

**Gill Rider** is the Head of the Civil Service Capability Group, a part of the Cabinet Office (UK).

Ms. Rider started her career in the financial markets, health-care, and government industries. She also worked in the customer service area examining industry best practices. She joined Accenture in 1979 and became a Partner in 1990. With operational responsibility for Accenture's Utilities practice in Europe and South Africa, she also served as Chairman of Accenture's United Kingdom and Ireland geographic unit. She then headed the European and Latin American operations of Accenture's Resources operating unit.

She became Accenture's Chief Leadership Officer when the position was created in March 2002. She headed the company's Organization and Leadership Development group, and was

## About the Contributors

responsible for developing the leadership capabilities and professional skills of Accenture's people and fostering a culture that encourages diversity and achievement.

Ms. Rider was appointed Director General, Leadership and People Strategy, at the Cabinet Office in February 2006. When Prime Minister Gordon Brown took office in June 2007, Ms. Rider continued in the Cabinet Office as Head of the Civil Service Capability Group. In this role she leads the Civil Service in transforming the professional skills of civil servants, developing leaders and promoting diversity. She also acts as Head of Profession for HR professionals across government, thereby building up the Service's HR capability.

In 2006 Ms. Rider became a Director for De La Rue, the world's largest commercial security printer and papermaker.

**John Roberts** is the former CEO of United Utilities.

Mr. Roberts graduated from Liverpool University and joined Manweb. After working his way up the company, he became Finance Director in 1984, then Managing Director in 1991. He was appointed Chief Executive a year later. He then became CEO of South Wales Electricity, being at the helm during its acquisition by Hyder, and was then appointed CEO of Hyder Utilities. He was appointed CEO of United Utilities in September 1999, and retired from the company in March 2006.

# About the Contributors

He is a former Director of Volex, a leading independent producer of electronic and fiber-optic cable assemblies and electrical power cords. He also served as the President of the Electricity Association and Chairman of the Electricity Pension Trustees Limited.

Mr. Roberts is currently a Director of International Power Plc. and the Royal Bank of Canada (Europe) Limited.

He is a Fellow of the Royal Academy of Engineering, the Institution of Electrical Engineers, and the Association of Chartered Certified Accountants.

**Dame Anita Roddick,** who passed away in September 2007, originally trained as a teacher. She then worked for the UN in Geneva before running a restaurant and hotel in Littlehampton, Sussex.

She started The Body Shop in Brighton in 1976 to create a livelihood for herself and her two daughters while her husband was trekking across the Americas. She had no training or experience, but economic necessity—combined with the colorful experiences she had gained from her various travels—saw the creation of a successful business dedicated to the pursuit of social and environmental change.

The Body Shop went public in 1984. It has grown from one store in England to a multinational company with nearly two thousand stores in fifty countries.

## About the Contributors

Anita Roddick became a Dame in July 2003 for services to retailing, the environment, and charity.

**Robin Ryde** is the former Chief Executive and Principal of the UK's National School of Government, a nonministerial department of the government that provides policy and management training for the UK Civil Service. Before taking on the role of Chief Executive, Mr. Ryde was the Head of the National School's Centre for Strategic Leadership.

Mr. Ryde spent three years at the Cabinet Office leading the Prime Minister's leadership development program—the Top Management Program, one of the largest leadership development programs in Europe. He also served as Director of Skills and Career Development at the National Audit Office, the nation's watchdog for government spending. In this position he was involved in leadership development, organizational change, and consultancy—in particular assisting U.K. and international government departments and smaller bodies to lead, deliver, and operate more efficiently.

He has led a variety of consultancy and "value for money" evaluations, ranging from the performance of Grant Maintained Schools, defense equipment acquisitions, and the sales of U.K. gold reserves, to programs tackling deprivation in Britain's poorest areas. Mr. Ryde has designed and delivered training in the United Kingdom and across South and North America on subjects ranging from creativity

## About the Contributors

to government reform, and from evaluation to accountability.

He is currently an independent consultant and author of the books *Thought Leadership* and *Custom-Built Leadership*.

**Laura Tyson** is a Professor and the former Dean of the Haas School of Business at the University of California at Berkeley. She is also a former Dean of the London Business School and a former White House National Economic Adviser.

Professor Tyson joined the London Business School in 2002 and left that position at the end of 2006. She was Dean of University of California at Berkeley's Haas School of Business from 1998 to 2001. From 1977 to 2001 she was a Professor of Economics, and from 1990 to 2001 she was a Professor of Business Administration at the University of California at Berkeley.

Professor Tyson served in the Clinton Administration from January 1993 to December 1996. Between February 1995 and December 1996 she served as the President's National Economic Adviser and was the highest-ranking woman in the Clinton White House. She was a key architect of President Clinton's domestic and international policy agenda during his first term in office. As the Administration's top economic adviser, she managed all economic policy-making throughout the executive branch.

## About the Contributors

Prior to this appointment Professor Tyson served as the sixteenth Chairman of the White House Council of Economic Advisers, the first woman to hold that post. Before joining the Clinton Administration, she published a number of books and articles on industrial competitiveness and trade, including the book *Who's Bashing Whom? Trade Conflict in High Technology Industries*.

Professor Tyson serves as Director on the boards of Morgan Stanley, Eastman Kodak Company, and AT&T (formerly Ameritech Corp).

## ACKNOWLEDGMENTS

First and foremost, a heartfelt thanks goes to all of the executives who have candidly shared their hard-won experience and battle-tested insights for the *Lessons Learned* series.

Angelia Herrin at Harvard Business Publishing has consistently offered unwavering support, good humor, and counsel from the inception of this ambitious project.

Brian Surette and David Goehring provided invaluable editorial direction, perspective, and encouragement, particularly for this second series. Many thanks to the entire HBP team of designers, copyeditors, and marketing professionals who helped bring this series to life.

Much appreciation goes to Jennifer Lynn and Christopher Benoît for research and diligent attention to detail, and to Roberto de Vicq de Cumptich for his imaginative cover designs.

Finally, thanks to our fellow cofounder James MacKinnon and the entire 50 Lessons team for the tremendous amount of time, effort, and steadfast support of this project.

**—Adam Sodowick and Andy Hasoon**
Directors and Cofounders, 50 Lessons

# THE LAST PAGE IS ONLY THE BEGINNING

## Watch Free *Lessons Learned* Video Interviews and Get Additional Resources

You've just read first-hand accounts from the business world's top leaders, but the learning doesn't have to end there. 50 Lessons gives you access to:

**Exclusive videos featuring the leaders profiled in this book**

**Practical advice for putting their insights into action**

**Challenging questions that extend your learning**

FREE ONLINE AT:
**www.50lessons.com/communicate**